AF471759

TIME IS

ROSA NEEDLEMAN

ISBN: 978-1-4834-7654-4 (sc)
ISBN: 978-1-4834-7653-7 (e)

Lulu Publishing Services rev. date: 10/31/2017

Contents

Calais

She was a teak and walnut sloop
Open deck, no motor
Twenty-one feet of hand-wrought
Promise

Her bowsprit evoked
Elegant schooners of a past
That wasn't ours to
Claim

We were new here still
Tuned to iron and concrete
Willing to enter a more fluid
Universe

Calais she was called
Did her maker know the story
The heartbreak of that historic
Name

We bought her, wed her to
The green Pacific,
Sluiced her down at dusk
Sold her with the dream

Someone else sailed her away
I still look for her

Caldera

Stand at the rim and peer down
    into the endless cleft in time
        dark enough to make you jellied at the brink.
where flaming rock once shot into the sky,
    a molten furnace exploding from within
        to carve a great hole in the earth.

Below, in the depths, hidden fire simmers with intent;
    restless with containment, it boils and bubbles
        ready to escape

Montana de Oro

Years beneath the roiled surface where cold black waters
    rest
two titans slid inevitably toward brute encounter
    thrust
upwards, the earth cracked, split, rose and fell,
    ripped
open the uterine walls of time to send out onto
    naked earth
great basalt cliffs to stand tower-strong with the weight
    of witness
to the struggle that left them cleft and wounded,
    stained
with their history and marooned in time

one could climb them like a staircase through the ages

Hopi Prayer for Rain

In the late dry afternoon, on each roof
    a dark shadow appears like smoke
        from a hidden fire
Each featureless face turns upward
    to the empty cloudless sky
        hands strain to beseech

The gathering below hushes to hear
    the chant that circles the earth
        and floats high to the sleeping gods
to wake them from sad dreams and beg
    that they will remember the land
        when they are moved to weep

Wait for the lone black cloud to cover the sun, the sky
        and flood the world

Ritual

On each flat roof on the mesa
there is a coop to hold the bird
captured in the early morning
before the law is up and alert
An eaglet taken from its nest
to serve, to heal, to carry a message
that the spirits will heed and thus,
there will be rain, the crops will not fail.

There is ceremony, honoring, prayer

Each brave in the kiva
seeks to fill the empty cage
with stolen glory.
And the eaglet must die.
Its parents bereft, circle and scream above
Black feathers litter the ground.
The skies promise nothing

The land is not cured with magic anymore.

Science

The silent grey box boasts long sterile corridors
    and doors refusing entry; behind them
unspeakable acts.

More powerful than gods crafting thunderbolts,
    men and machines collude to alter
the universe.

A blind kitten bumps against the wall and turns
    and turns again and again seeking
an exit.

She wears a little helmet made to cover
    her fragile skull; like any alien visitor
she's lost

Did you know the auditory system of a cat
    is similar to a human's; a fortunate gift
for science

The kitten hears but no longer sees
    the hairless monkeys shivering
in their cages

I close my eyes and hear nothing
    behind my closed door; I stay out of
the corridors

Cured

Content with herself, so smooth as if
She had been pressed through a sieve, her
Jagged edges shaved off to fit the small openings,
So smooth a sort of porridge resulted, bland and tasteless.

"Years of therapy", she crowed, "changed my persona.
I'm OK now. I don't get angry anymore.."

I had not known who she was before,
With her passions and her angers
Missed them all the same and wondered
About the what and why of the discarded parts.

In her religion one must be buried unaltered.
She cannot realize
Having lived stripped, she will go into the ground empty

Mothers

There are mothers wearing aprons,
    holding mixing bowls
exhaling warmth and comfort with each breath
cushioning with love the hardships
    of fledging and flying .
Acceptance swells their eyelids.
They feed their young from a full larder.

And the others, unsung, whose aprons
    hold only cracked bowls.
They lie awake all night worrying:
would there be enough – good enough?
The stove is cold.
The cupboard always half empty.

Fairfax Avenue Comida

The burrito, petito burrito
 has muscled its way
  into Saul's deli,
   signaling a change of scene.

Gone, the payess, long black coat,
fur hat of the ultra-Orthodox.

The new religioso is young,
 wears its pants below the butt crack
  eats a different dish of la vida:
   menudo with a side of Madonna
   or a hot sauce of Santeria

The tide washes in and out
The sand
   does not maintain

Collateral Damage

A fly, black tear, rests on her cheek
Child face, gaunt and fearful
        will never grow into lost beauty
Child heart will never still its wild beating
Old in youth, lifespan foretold
        by unlucky chance of birthplace
The barren fields cannot nurture the present
Though they are heavy with blood and bones
Those who remain feast on weeds and wind
The child missed – by a continent –
        hopscotch, hide and seek
        life.

Time is

The clock reads nine or almost nine or just after nine
The watch claims nine-oh-five or maybe seven
Although it was twinned to the heartbeat of the clock
A gift – five minutes, seven – of found time to use as needed
Stuff the seconds with the possible
Until the pretence of "if" becomes the reality of "now"

Pull it long and fit in all the living you must do
Malleable time, stretched like elastic
The moments are forgiving but not endlessly so
Careful! Lest the boundaries dissolve;
The playful eddies become a whirlpool
And fling you into "never"

Universe

The afternoon was sunlit and remote
  from life below in the foothills.
After the color left the side of the building
  behind our chair backs
And settled into the grass beneath our feet,
Poppies sprang from the wet earth still smelling
  of paint.
Caves appeared, dark maws gaping in invitation.
I read a koan in the black and white crow,
  wings covering the sky
and heard the heartbeat of a strawberry
  cupped in the palm of my hand
Watched as the ribbon of time unfolded

Slowly made my way back to an alternate universe.

White Lilies

Strange that brides carry white lilies,
churches present them in huge arrays
on the corners of the altar.
They are a flower of great austerity,
erect and forthright
they do not charm; they insist.

We have misunderstood their message;
they speak of death,
they bear the pain of loss,
they are best seen on a coffin.

White, the death of innocence;
white, the end of purity
White is the shroud in which we bury life.
Lilies speak of farewell

Little Friend

Little friend, awkwardly shaped
How can I love you, you who lack
The charm and delight of your kind
You, with a balloon of a body, a rasp of a voice

Yet, I do love you

I love you because you are mine,
Because you need me

"He was always a good boy" she lies
The sullen, acne-scarred adolescent destroyed
All her half-formed hopes
Broke all the rules and her heart

Yet she forgives him

She forgives the baby she nursed
He will always need her

Loving the loveable – so easy – like
Singing a song with no sharps or flats
The discordant, too, must be loved

Guilty

…..he reached for his……

…I feared for my….

life – had to shoot him..

You say no gun…

must have ditched it….

…only 14? But…

probably dealing ..

Betcha on crack….

Little bastard

…spoil the city..

…no respect for life…

I'm OK

It's my job

Red Brick

A letter from a friend warns me not to visit
The lovely ivy-covered buildings of my college
have been leveled to make room
for The School of Business Admin, the School of Performing
Arts, The School of Architecture

The red brick has been replaced by glass and steel
Ivy does not grow on such slick surfaces
The grassy areas and arbors are parking lots
Shadowed arcades along the library shade no longer
The koi pool, too costly to maintain, removed

Where does one go now to sit in the autumn colors
And dream of afterwards?

Creek

Algae covers the still water of the creek
The Golden-eye too is still
hoping for
                a promising ripple

She is alone, far from her fly way

She is lost and the dead water will not
                sustain her
Scrub, weeds, marsh grass line the bank
a hidden wilderness full
                of small, humming creatures

Joggers pass – neither see nor hear

Playa Vista

Built on a marsh
Once egrets tiptoed daintily here
Lifting their slender legs to leave no ripple
        in the water
Now, drained, tamed, emptied of life
There are concrete bunkers laced with iron-work balconies

The walkways stretch out at rigid angles
The grass mowed into well-trimmed stubble
On the lamp posts a container of plastic bags
Lest the dog's waste sully the landscape

Hushed corridors and closed doors
Behind them the elders growing older
Like the egrets
They will leave the water undisturbed
In time the tall grass will return

Cell Phone

What happens when the phone rings
And no one answers
when the text flies out
and lands in an empty room

In silence, the message aborts

What might have been is not
will not happen
The loneliness of the unheard ringing
The useless unread words

The spinning orb stops briefly

Resumes unchanged

Flora

We are always ourselves
in different guises
wearing different colors
turning and swaying
to wind-driven music

lit by sunlight or drowned in darkness
sheltered by green surround

We are ourselves as we bud
as we slowly unfold
as we are rained upon
nibbled by insects
browned at the edges by age

until we drop with the exhaustion
of having lived

Silence

Just once more
Let us speak of it
Once more before
We bury it with silence
Before we turn away
And – unresolved – the issue
Tunnels deep beneath
The skins of the unspoken
Words that separate and tie us

From unheard whispers
Grows a thick forest of silent cries
We cannot find our way out
Every turn further into the dark growth
Every breath a final sigh

Noise

In the darkness, a rustle
The slightest rustle
A gentle noise, a tentative noise

I heard it in my sleep
I heard it through the dream I was dreaming
That gruff, light sound under the silence

The cat, the dog
One or the other settling into the night
A soft rustle to comfort me with presence

Names

Do not speak my name
Do not call me into being
Magic is not strong enough to summon me

I do not wish to be what I am named
I will not answer; I have hidden from myself and you
My name is a curse that dooms me
        to live in your world

I would be else
Live in a garden
Do no evil

I fear the fate that knows my path
That waits for my naked self to answer the call
Binds me to myself for sins uncommitted

I will await my own annointed vision
I will borrow another self with a clean name
I will be born again

For You

Here I am in my rosa-ness
Waiting to give myself to you
I have form, favor, color
You may have me in rose red or apricot,
        pink,purple
Do not choose me in white
I have been sadly soiled and damaged
While I waited for you to want me

A rose fades fast
Petals curl inward
Scent lost
A waste, a death
Unless you pluck me, water me, nurture me
Keep me alive for a little while longer

Migrant

In a prop plane – before jets were ordinary
I turned my face to the window and wept
and wept for all the hours of the long flight
on my way west to join a man who waited.

This man I had happily parted from a year ago
had left to start a new life in the California myth while
I tried to make it on my own in the old, known world.

A man without grace; a place without pleasure,
spindly palms, concrete boxes with cat walks
This my new home. "Only gypsies roam" a warning
that new roots would be shallow and sickly.

This, then, defeat and escape and migration to
An unwanted refuge.

The sun sets in the west

Morning

We pass each other each day in the early morning hour of five.
He is in a three-piece suit, I think –
- it is still too dark to see details
And carries a large satchel.
I wear a long red raincoat over my robe
And unlaced boots; a veritable bag lady.

This opening act of the day is a small mystery
Who is this man
Where does he go – on foot?
Why this daily early departure?

We acknowledge each other briefly with a nod
And what does he think of me, dressed so oddly?

The dog and I watch as he disappears into the morning.

Ride

The train takes off without my noticing,
slides down the track swaying
only a little side to side.
All I need do is bend
my knees and let my body
move.

Stations glide by promising
adventure, danger; I let them pass.
My feet root, hands clutch the pole.
The stranger behind me shoves me
out the door and into
chaos.

Surgery

Since July I have had a new body
    from the waist up
Square, concave, featureless, more
    like a block of wood
Scarred by irregular lines grooved into the surface

There is something inert, halted, unfinished
    about the look
though once there were breasts,
two, proper hillocks on the fleshy plain

Gone - Lost
Nothing to admire under a winter sweater or summer dress
No invitation to touch, fondle, caress, whispers softly
No pleasure in the mirror's story

But the rest of me resides in what is left of me

Paean to the Body

I can't rely on the old bod anymore:
The intake/output mechanism doesn't work seamlessly;
Odd messages of pain find their way from nerve to brain;
Outcroppings of unnecessary flesh appear hear and there;
And inside, well, stuff grows where stuff shouldn't grow and
has to be sawn off like a rotten branch.

Can't count on early to bed and early to rise making me wise
Early to bed, sure....past eight words by-pass
the brain
No reason to keep the eyes working to take in the world
Early to rise, well...lumber, strain..."rise" is such a light, painless word
No longer really descriptive of the action at start of day.

Wish I'd liked you more when I had you whole, old bod
Wish I'd looked in the mirror and celebrated you daily
Grateful now for your creaky willingness to plow on and
carry me where I need to go
Until I don't need to go anywhere at all.

Secrets

My DNA codes for secrecy.

I am a descendant of a long line of strangers
resistant to their own histories
they remembered little, shared even less
with their children, the inheritors of untold stories
Lost, the past, the present, the future
Too late – we ask nothing
We do not know the questions.
Something, someone needs protection.

What can have happened? The curtain rose;
the actors spoke their lines, exited –
no incest, no murder; a script of loss, loneliness, hope,
disappointment – written on tissue
A photo album offers clues, actors:
friends, partners, lovers, long gone with their stories;
fading now into sepia.
No substance remaining, we conjure, invent, imagine
There is no mystery.

There is only mystery.

The Greeks

Not statues, my Greeks move, did move, did present their bodies;
now in my gallery of former lovers, still flesh, still warm
each better than marble David motionless in time and so
useless in bed.

I woke late, opened later, budding slowly and reluctantly
afraid to know my own colors, afraid to know theirs
the first, boy/man, sweet below the waist; surprising riches between his legs
too young to feast well on that gift, I wasted it, not wanting it.

The lean sage who tuned me like a harp, whose name I have forgotten-
call him Epicurus – awakened in me a new hunger
and we gorged until he was sated, left the table
leaving me wanting more.

Ah, the comfortable man, Roman perhaps, not hesitant, not cautious;
endowed by the gods with young vitality, rough energy,
bulky and armored in clothes, stripped, his beauty revealed
all the weight and heft of him there for my pleasure

And the others. My body remembers them all – their flesh, their desires;
the shape of their warmth enfolding me
like a summer quilt resting on legs, breasts, belly;
the penis within me – ferocious, demanding, giving, wanting release.

The hour is late.
I am not tired.
The corridors are deserted.

Love's Labour

When she spoke to him, her tongue stabbed like nettles
When he touched her, her spines pierced his hands
He could not embrace her for fear of being impaled
He could not comfort her without armour

How then to love her?

The wall surrounding her rose high in brick and mortar
To climb over? To look for chinks or take a hammer
And attack the edifice?
Then face the next line of defense.

A heavy labour for love.

One could not know how she thirsts for it
Alone in the desert that surrounds her
Only the spiney cactus witness
The silent plea: risk, risk, climb – forgive

Lost love's labour

Momento Mori

Almost over
Will I be remembered?
More to the point, will I be honored?
It's too late to be cherished.
If it's happened, I don't think I know.
So, value for time spent – not just here
And gone.

Where is my mark?
No TV until after 4;
6 books a week,
Funny, smart.
Not unkind, uncool, uncaring.
Not good enough.

The train for Syracuse left hours ago.
The bike has a flat tire.
In her dreams, running, the cat's paws
Rake the air.
Me too; running, backward to start again.

Inheritance

We didn't get along, psyches rubbing abrasively,
setting the room electric with negative vibration;
so why did my father invite me into his office to
sit and work alongside him that summer?
And why did I accept the offer – so that today
what I remember: I was there; he was there
It was OK.

Years later he would walk me into a law library,
his guest in the structure of his world.
I sat in a black leather chair, books stacked
in front of me on a high oak table
and felt I had come to my home.

Veteran

The highlight of his life was his service in the Great War
Nothing before or since matched those few flaming years
    with strangers he called brothers
The remaining peaks and valleys of his existence were
    yearly meetings of those grey men hanging fast
    and the funerals of those who had let go.

Once a year – Memorial Day – wives fastened ribbons of
    remembrance and regret
    on too tight jackets with battalion shoulder patches
    old division numbers on the collars
And the dwindling few marched slowly down 5th Avenue
Steps somewhat shakey and breath coming hard.

Looking back on those long-gone glory days sustained
    his slow reluctant ageing
Marriage, fatherhood, career – uncelebrated;
    merely traffic stops on a well-mapped road
    nothing to photograph for the family album
He lived his life as if in a featureless landscape until

    He, too, let go

Sunday Story

My petite mother hides in the kitchen while
her four tall brothers fill all the space outside.
Five o'clock or so on Sunday each week
they unexpectedly invade, uninvited,
always welcome, always a disaster.

Mother wrings her hands at the sink
What to do? Will they want dinner?
She has nothing to cook – unprepared again
as she was last week and the one before.
How is this a surprise, this Sunday?

She is the eldest, was just as overwhelmed
in her girlhood, when, uninvited, one after another,
aliens took over her world and, with complete kindness
and even love, pushed her from its center.
She does not really want to serve.

We all go out for Chinese food.

Not There

She would not, could not, walk upright – raise her head, pull her shoulders back and stride
How sad, hushed and insecure, she melted into the landscape of her life.
So much missed: choices, decisions, satisfactions.
Green was the color of the year; green was the color of her carpet.
Dinners spoiled; had she cooked the roast too long, not long enough?
Thank heavens no one special was invited to dine
No one ever invited to dine
Her family the only witness to her muted whimpers.
No comforting had on her shoulder'
The next time no better than the last.

The Critic

"Good looks are not your forte", she said,
as we shared a mirror.
Of course she meant well. I was to use
my other talents to charm, to engage.
What remained all the years - - were the words;
stones lodged in the gut.
A gift out of Grimm, she possessed, an evil blessing.
Her mouth opened for an exodus of frogs;
and they live, hopping about in memory.
Like Medea, in all innocence, she said,
        "I never"

How I remember her

Carved wooden face, stranger to a smile;
long black hair
coarse and abundant over her shoulders
as she combed all the mystery from it
each morning to smother it
in a tight, cruel bun.

Flat, silent eyes barring entry
to her thoughts,
her hopes, so long buried;
door closed to her heart;
taut, spare body held rigidly
from embrace.

She did not nurture;
could not.
The food she cooked – flavorless
The stories she held – meaningless
Too much history choked
the soft corners of her life.

What she could have been

Mirror Mirror

The mirror over the dresser blazed her image back at the world.
It moved to our apartment when I married her son.
Even together we could not mute her;
She sang out in C major and, in all the major and minors, she commanded:
  "Billy eat your peas." "Sandy, stand up straight."
  "Where's my mascara?"
  "No baby on the way yet?"
  "Ben, it's late; let's go."

I looked for me in that glass but see only her,
Blonded, powdered, mascaraed.
We cleaned and dusted, even windexed regularly
But she shone brightly and irreversibly.
We gave her to Goodwill.
Someone else has her now.

That Sunday

In the early morning dark
  a flight of narrow stairs
At the bottom, a landing where
  the Sunday Times should lie
  awaiting collection
At the top, the kitchen, spare,
  the usual equipment and a
  table and 4 chairs
where no one is sitting.

When the Times does not appear this morning
  someone will walk to the corner market
  to buy it, looking past the sleeping windows of
  ice cream parlor and dry cleaners
  deaf to the silent street.

Standing in the square room
  at the top of the stairs
  pencil in hand
  poised for the crossword puzzle, he waits.
She cleans the breakfast mess away
  postponing conversation;
Quiet wraps around the long moments.

The front door remains closed still;
  no steps are heard
  in the stairwell.
The kitchen clock whispers softly.
Grey shadows slide into the corners.
Sunday fades into dusk.

Someone does not return.
The morning disappears into time.

The Cypress

The cypress outside my bedroom window greens upward yearly
But the new growth surrounds a center rotten with decay,
Black, loamy and hiding a secret life.

An ancient raccoon, massive with age, awaits his end there.
He rests alone on a bed of soft needles.
Chattering squirrels look in on him daily

Spiders weave a curtain to soften the sun's glare
Crickets sacrifice to feed his occasional hunger.
He cannot number his awakenings

His memories have deserted him
His body a grey shell
He no longer ventures out in search of life

A blanket of dusk brings quiet comfort.
Soon his night will be permanent.
But I have seen him and I will not forget.

Shelter Dog

They wait each morning, the lost and found: fox-faced chihuauas,
Bright terriers, the bully breeds, the mixed, the mutts.
Cacophany of fierce demand, their cries an assault,
Their bodies fevered with impatience
And yes, their souls. No one could deny them such status
Who knows them, each being friend in need of honor and respect
They know me too – only as jailor
And release.

While escorting some quivering dog for his morning walk
The two of us talk; I say "good dog, good boy" and he studies me,
Reads my face, my eyes, to see if I am sincere.
Reassured, he tugs the leash to signal: time to walk on,
Sniff the sidewalk, watch the cars rush by, pee in precisely
The right spot right there against the lamp post, not least,
If he's lucky, snatch a taste of a homeless man's meager
Breakfast feast.

We head for home, a noisy kennel in a shelter for his kind:
The abandoned, unwanted, inconvenient animal detritus
Of our busy lives. I hope he will not be waiting tomorrow.
Someone will have seen the promise of love he offers ; he
Will have a new home, a better friend than I have been.
I will walk another dog up and down a few city blocks;
Out from the sheltered, barred cage for a brief, temporary
Prison break.

Walking the Dog

Time is fashioned into pie – slices of pie
    Four-hour slice – a bit skimpy
    The dog isn't quite ready to go
    A six-hour slice is heavy
    The dog dances a bit as
I slip the braided leash around her neck

And we walk while I contemplate the next slice
    Shall I cut it fine or fat
    The day is eaten up in chunks
    This one, barely done; the next looming
    No rest, not a release
She needs, I respond, and thus we bond

Newcomer

The little white cat from next door
has begun to pay me visits
I find her in the stairwell waiting to play
she has a grey widow's peak on her head
giving her a sage and worried look
perhaps she is thinking of her home back in Detroit
and wondering if the weather in Los Angeles will suit her
if the streets are safe for her wanderings

I want to take her in and cosset her
protect her from her instincts
but I see she needs her freedom
to risk and retreat
needs to find her own comfort

as I need her grace and blessing

Ryon

The absence of his presence, a palpable void
        marks each day
The hand remembers the long, bony skull,
golden fur, softer than a whisper

The slow leak of the body's blood
like sand in the hourglass falling by seconds
stains the street, claiming the place Ryon filled

There remains only margins and surround leaving
        the empty space that is
Once was composed of daily experience – skin, bone, muscle
now removed from all possibility

Elegy for Mini

Black hole in the center of my life
Can't get too close or I'm sucked in like
    a piece of earthly flotsam – or is it jetsam?
Small shadow in the carpet.
Nothing there – with tail held high.
Don't look too long or nothing
    will appear.
Atoms coalesce to stretch
    a living body in the space left empty.
Was but is no more and the world
smaller, sadder without beloved friend

The Calico Cat

The calico cat is not
Unaware of her tri-colored beauty
Preens quietly and with great discretion
Knowing some fool will be enticed
By amber eyes.

Snow coat embellished by silks
Black, brown, orange, disguise
Her subtle, perfidious feline being

Careful, she is enchantress
If you stare at her with desire
She has won.
You will love her and you will serve her until
Her colors fade and her golden eyes close.

She has returned to her world.

Zoo

The pangolin, the sloth, armadillo and platypus
All pranks of Nature
How she jokes!
  Silvery armor for the gentle giant
  Fur to house fungi in a beast that inches
  A tongue longer than its body sweeps up lunch
  Poor confused soul: duck-billed, egg-laying, unable to decide
    Am I mammal or not mammal

But Mother N has not run out of steam
Best joke for last
A special animal:
  Walks on two legs, talks, pronounces, pontificates, boasts:
  I can, therefore I will
  I am, therefore I am, ergo ego

About the Author

Rosa Needleman is a former Professor of Linguistics and ESL, now retired, with a passion for animals, music and poetry. She has been in poetry workshops and has contributed to several anthologies of poetry. These poems were written over the past few years.

www.ingramcontent.com/pod-product-compliance
Ingram Content Group UK Ltd.
Pitfield, Milton Keynes, MK11 3LW, UK
UKHW041838200726
13854UKWH00003BA/1208

9 781483 47654